PEGASUS ENCYCLOPEDIA

TRUCKS

Edited by: Pallabi B. Tomar
Managing editor: Tapasi De
Designed by: Vijesh Chahal and Nirbhay Kumar
Illustrated by: Suman S. Roy, Tanoy Choudhury
Colouring done by: Vinay Kumar, Sonu, Kiran Kumari & Pradeep Kumar

TRUCKS

CONTENTS

Introduction 3

History 4

Types of trucks 7

Parts of a truck 10

Maintenance of trucks 14

Advantages 18

Disadvantages 19

Trucking industry 20

Famous truck manufacturers 23

Some famous trucks 26

Test Your Memory 31

Index 32

Introduction

Truck, derived from the Greek word 'trochos' meaning 'wheel' is a vehicle that carries goods and materials. While there are luxury cars to carry people around, there are trucks that carry large and heavy goods and materials from one place to another.

Unlike automobiles, which usually have a unibody construction, most trucks are built around a strong frame called a **chassis**. They come in all sizes, from the automobile-sized pickup truck to towering off-road mining trucks or heavy highway semi-trailers.

There are trucks that use gasoline engines, while other trucks use four stroke turbo intercooler diesel engines. Some trucks also use locomotive-type engines. There are military-type light trucks that are used for troop transport.

The term is most commonly used in American English and Australian English to refer to what earlier was called a motor truck, and in British English is often called a lorry or for bigger vehicles, a Heavy Goods Vehicle (HGV). This type of truck is a motor vehicle designed to carry goods, with a cab and a tray or compartment for carrying goods.

Industrial designer Viktor Schreckengost revolutionized the trucking industry in 1932 when he redesigned the standard truck's body by placing the cab right over the engine.

TRUCKS

History

As there were attempts to innovate machines to transport goods other than steam engines in the second half of the eighteenth century, what can be described as the first truck in history was born in 1896.

Built by Daimler-Motoren-Gesellschaft, the initial design was derived from the carts of the time, simply by removing the front of the animals intended for hooking and pulling with the assembly of the wheel axles of a two-cylinder engine for about 2200 cm3 which developed 6 horsepower and could propel the vehicle at a speed of 16 km/ h. The wheels were strictly made of wood with the outer rim of metal and also the braking system was the same used for the coaches.

Following the evolution of cars, manufacturers improved with the adoption of a closed body that protects the driver. The engine was positioned in front of the cockpit. Another important improvement concerns the transition to solid rubber tyres and the presence of the first diversification of the receptacles, now closed.

In the first two decades of the twentieth century the importance of trucks continued to increase. Other manufacturers were impoverished in the market, such as Fiat, which provided the first truck to the Royal Army, Fiat 15. The end of the twenties saw the first trucks equipped with shaft drive and the first equipped with tyres tube.

The Ford truck was introduced in 1925 after more than a 20 years research by Henry Ford.

History

Ford trucks have been the most consistent best selling vehicle for the Ford Motor Company.

The innovations introduced in the thirties were also very important for the continuation of the history of the truck. First, the engine, until then positioned behind the front axle, was taken much further in front and on the same axis, resulting in an immediate best weight distribution on the truck and a substantial increase in payload. The wooden wheels were in the meantime, completely abandoned in favour of metal wheels and brakes, until then limited usually to the front wheels, it also widened the rear of the vehicle. In the cities trucks made more and more deliveries. Even the engines were moving increasingly towards petrol and diesel.

The following decade saw the truck again at the centre of attention mainly for its work in the field of war. During the Second World War, it was the main vehicle for the transfer of troops and baggage on the various fronts and all the branch companies were engaged in manufacturing it to meet the huge demand which cropped up during that time.

After the World War II, companies returned again to design vehicles for civilian use. More and more trucks equipped with diesel engines hit the market, a remarkable step forward in energy.

TRUCKS

In the fifties the first engine had a turbocharger, and they had powers of average around 200 horsepower. Perhaps the only thing that had made great strides was taking care of its interior cabins, especially with regard to the acoustic and thermal insulation of the passenger. With the first movement of the driver directly above the engine room, driving conditions were certainly not favourable, especially in the warmer months of the year.

The importance of the driver was taken seriously only in later years with the study of new solutions to make the driving time as comfortable as possible. Among the solutions found were those of a higher thermal and sound insulation, a more ergonomic design of seats and using the power steering, anti-vibration supports the inclusion of suspension system between the cab and chassis, together with the emergence of the cabins and the presence of a bed room behind the seats allowing the driver to stay in overnight stops.

The seventies and eighties saw the research in the field of the driver's visibility to the outside, the introduction of rigid bars on the sides and rear to prevent other vehicles to be able to slide under the truck in an accident, the introduction of disc brakes more powerful and the presentation of the first air suspension that significantly improved the ride attitude.

In these same years also developed a technology that allowed carriers to remain in contact with each other and sometimes even their homes. It was very useful to report problems on the roads. Now almost all trucks for long journeys were fitted with a radio transceiver, the famous CB.

The last decade of the century saw an increasing emphasis on the ecological impact and the manufacturers devoted much of their ability to start engine production with fewer emissions and pollutants.

Astonishing fact

In the early days of the fire service, fire trucks were horse drawn. In those days nearly every firehouse had a resident Dalmatian. The job of the Dalmatian was to lead the horses to the fire and protect them from horse thieves.

Types of trucks

Haulage Trucks

Haulage trucks are heavy duty carriers used to carry parcels, courier and for logistics. Some are used to transport cars, two-wheelers and three-wheelers, bricks, sand and coal or as water/petrol tankers.

Rigid Trucks

Rigid trucks are sturdy and used as transit mixers, containers, acid tankers, recovery trucks, self-loading cranes and even as liquefied petroleum gas containers.

Tippers

Tippers are robust vehicles used for tipping operations in industries such as construction and building, mining and quarrying industry and the public service sector. They can be used for on or off-highway needs.

Dump Trucks

A dump truck or production truck is a truck used for transporting loose material (such as sand, gravel, or dirt) for construction. A typical dump truck is equipped with a hydraulically operated open-box bed hinged at the rear, the front of which can be lifted up to allow the contents to be deposited on the ground behind the truck at the site of delivery. They are used by municipal corporations and the building industry.

TRUCKS

Pickup Trucks

The capacity of this vehicle is limited to 788 kg. The number of items that can be loaded is eight at a maximum. It is usually used for payload items. It is mainly used for business purposes which includes the transportation of electronic products or products that are heavy and big.

Flatbed Trucks

A flatbed truck is a type of truck which can be either articulated or rigid. It has an entirely flat, level body with absolutely no sides or roof. This allows for quick and easy loading of goods, and consequently they are used to transport heavy loads that are not delicate or vulnerable to precipitation, such as construction equipment, and also for abnormal loads that require more space than is available on a closed body. Trucks of this type are considered ideal for transporting goods that need to be unloaded quickly from the sides as well as the rear.

Garbage Trucks

A Waste Collection Vehicle (WCV) is a truck specially designed to pick up smaller quantities of waste and haul it to landfills and other recycling or treatment facilities. They are a common sight in most urban areas.

Types of trucks

Panel Trucks

A panel truck is a windowless cargo van built on a truck chassis. It is a station wagon with no backseat and no side windows behind the front doors. They are frequently used for delivery of flowers, retail bakery products, diapers, laundry and other consumer conveniences.

Semi-Trailer Trucks

A semi-trailer truck is an articulated truck or lorry consisting of a towing engine (tractor in the U.S., prime mover in Australia, and truck in UK, Canada and New Zealand), and a semi-trailer (plus possible additional trailers) that carries the freight.

> Volvo trucks are currently sold in more than 140 countries all over the world, but it all began with the first one rolling off the assembly line in 1928 in Sweden.

Tanker Trucks

A tanker truck is a motor vehicle designed to carry liquefied loads, dry bulk cargo or gasses on roads. The largest such vehicles are similar to railroad tank cars which are also designed to carry liquefied loads. Many variants exist due to the wide variety of liquids that can be transported. Tank trucks tend to be large; they may be insulated or non-insulated, pressurized or non-pressurized and designed for single or multiple loads (often by means of internal divisions in their tank).

Parts of a truck

Chassis

A truck chassis consists of two parallel U-shaped beams held together by cross members. It is usually made of steel, but can be made (whole or in part) of aluminium for a lighter weight. The chassis is the main structure of the truck, and the other parts are attached to it.

> During World War II, Volvo was a main supplier to the Swedish Armed Forces, and thousands of their 'Roundnose' trucks were used in military operations.

Cab

The cab is an enclosed space where the driver is seated. A sleeper is a compartment attached to the cab where the driver can rest while not driving. They can range from a simple 24" (0.6 m) bunk to a 120" (3.0 m) apartment-on-wheels.

Modern cabs feature air conditioning, a good sound system, and ergonomic seats (often air suspended).

Engine

Trucks can use all sorts of engines. Small trucks such as SUVs or pickups and even light medium-duty trucks use gasoline engines. Heavier trucks use four stroke turbo diesel engines, although there are alternatives. Huge off-highway trucks use locomotive-type engines such as a V12 Detroit Diesel two stroke engine.

Parts of a truck

Seats

In general, the vehicle is equipped with one or two seats for any passenger beside the driver. In recent years, however, manufacturers have approved models capable of carrying more people, sleepers up to nine. The Italian law provides that on board the truck there can only be the driver and persons directly related to loading and unloading of cargoes; therefore, these passengers cannot be compared to those of cars.

The driver's seat of a truck must always be protected from any movement of objects carried. This is achieved by keeping separate the cab from the cargo area or applying a protective partition behind the driver in case of a single body compartment.

The classic truck is one in which the cargo space, whether it be van tarpaulin, is completely separated from the cockpit.

The truck frames are provided with a variable number of drive gear, usually 2 or 3 for the most common uses, and the engine is usually equipped with wheels. The more modern are equipped with air springs that provide the means to an optimum level regardless of load carried and also allow a more comfortable ride.

> **The Volvo FH is the most successful range of trucks Volvo has ever built. In 2000, the FH12 was awarded the 'Truck of the Year.'**

TRUCKS

The engines currently produced are strictly diesel. The drive gear is a mechanical lever, while the gearbox is generally controlled by a button on the gear knob itself. In heavy vehicles, especially those used for towing trailers or semitrailers, the change typically consists of a box base, which is typically 3 or 4 gears plus reverse, and a range selector gear places respectively downstream and upstream of case basis.

The truck loading areas of common use are characterized by a width that easily allows you to load the goods on pallets, typically 240 cm, with a base level and made of wood or aluminium. The effective height for the load is around 280 cm in the most modern methods available to low-frame chassis and suspension. The vehicle has an average length of about 6 m, but useful, reaching the maximum permitted overall limit. There are even boxes with lengths up to 10/10, 5 m (12 ft to stay in total, about 2 m cabin + 10 m of body).

Even for the transport of dangerous goods (ADR) the approval for the cargo is subject to certain conditions.

There must be fire resistant materials for the cover that covers the outside and must indicate on the cargo marking the type of goods being transported and the nature of the hazard. Tables of the same type must be indicated on the sides and front of the car, outside the cab. In addition, vehicles carrying dangerous goods must have a specific setting which consists of shielded electrical cables and connections.

Parts of a truck

For stability and safety during the lifting of materials through the crane, which must be strictly stationary, is equipped with 4 independent outriggers, hydraulic controls, to adapt to every shape of land and prevent dangerous movements of the load being handled.

A device in a truck called a 'switch' allows you to isolate the battery from the rest of the vehicle by turning on a switch.

Presence of equipment for fire-fighting is a must and the crew of the vehicle must know the use. The fire extinguishers must meet a recognized standard and be sealed to ensure that they are not used. The date by which the next inspection should take place should also be mentioned.

The most common use is for the loading of diggers, bulldozers, forklifts etc and for deliveries of heavy materials in places where there are no loading docks and appropriate equipments (e.g. construction sites).

TRUCKS

Maintenance of trucks

Fluid checks

Trucks use a fair amount of fluids to perform its everyday tasks. So, it is important you check the fluids regularly. Check the fluids once a month. The fluids include the brake fluid, coolant, oil and power steering fluid. It is best to check the oil once the engine has warmed up for 10 minutes. Oil expands as it cools and constricts as it heats up, so you will get the most accurate reading when the engine is warm. When you buy your truck, whether it is new or used, make sure you have an owner's manual. It will tell you what type of fluids to use and what the maintenance schedule for the truck should be.

Changing the oil is probably the best insurance you can have to keep a truck running better and longer. Schedules vary from manufacturer to manufacturer, but this does not take into consideration the extra work expected out of your truck. Opinions vary, but it is a safe bet that if you change the oil every 3 to 4 thousand kilometres and change the filter in the process, your vehicle will last much longer. Often, a delivery vehicle spends a lot of time in stop and go traffic, and will spend more time idling than a normal vehicle. For this reason, the oil breaks down quicker. Changing often and using a good grade of motor oil saves a lot of wear and tear.

Maintenance of trucks

Advanced maintenance

If driving a heavy-duty truck, grease the moving parts in the truck's engine weekly. Change the fluids and power components in your vehicle according to the hours you are driving. The oil should be changed every 250 hours of driving, while the automatic transmission fluid and the standard transmission fluid should be changed every 500 and 1000 hours, respectively. The rear differentials, a component of your trucks axle, should have its fluid changed every 600 hours; the power steering, what makes the truck turn easily even though it weighs more than a ton, should have its fluid changed every 1600 km.

Extras

Add extras to your engine to keep it running efficiently, such as fluid add-ons that aid performance. Add engine coolant to your hydraulic system to keep engine running heat low, it extends the life of your engine. Add fluid called an additive to your gasoline tank, to get better gas mileage and to keep your fuel pipes clean.

Tyre and brakes

Besides the engine of the truck, the next two things that really make it run well are the tyres and the brakes. The brakes should be always functioning perfectly and accurately. The brakes not working well can put you in a very vulnerable and dangerous position.

15

TRUCKS

Tyres need to be rotated on a regular basis to insure even wear. When tyres are rotated, it gives the mechanic an opportunity to check brakes and brake lines and look for abnormal wear. Also very important to the life of your tyres is checking the air pressure on a weekly basis. Remember that tyre pressures are focused on two things— a smoother ride and better stability. When considering that you maybe carrying loads that are a great deal more than an average vehicle, you may want to think about raising the tyre pressure a bit over the manufacturer's suggestions. Remember that a tyre that is low on air pressure generates a great deal more heat. Heat is the biggest enemy of a tyre, allowing it to wear out faster. Also, decreased tyre pressure, especially when hauling a load, can cause the vehicle to be much less stable than usual. Better to check the tyre pressure on a weekly basis than to have an accident.

Check suspension components and shocks on a regular basis. Because they bear more weight, they wear quicker. Poor suspension means a rough and dangerous ride, especially when carrying a load. It isn't uncommon for a load to shift if the shocks are not up to par.

Any abnormal sounds from the truck should be checked out immediately without wasting any time.

Repair and maintenance

Ensure that at the truck maintenance, everything is checked thoroughly by a

Maintenance of trucks

professional mechanic. Even something as inconsequential as lights are extremely important as they go on to alert the other drivers about the presence of the truck. Lights are quite easy to break, get cracked or not be working. Ensure that they are in the best of working conditions.

Signals and mirrors

These are the other things in your truck that will ensure your driving safety. A truck needs the right aid of turning signals in order to let the other drivers know about its next step. Also, the mirrors will allow the driver to be able to see what is behind them and the kind of traffic around them. This will make them feel more in control of driving the truck.

Battery

Periodic maintenance of the truck will ensure that the battery is working perfectly so as to allow you to be able to use the fuel optimally without any wastage.

Modern trucks have a lot more features now than in previous decades. Onboard computers allow your maintenance man to keep a closer eye on what is going on with the engine, and a lot of sensors are now used to keep an eye on such things as exhaust emission and vacuum modules. Even with all this, however, it is a necessity to keep an eye on things from both a visual view and through regularly scheduled maintenance.

Advantages

The importance of the trucking industry is rising. Trucks can access remote and hilly areas where rail lines cannot be constructed. The trucking industry enables quick, easy departure of goods and accepts smaller loads than railways.

A truck is unique because it has an open cargo bed that allows easy access for carrying large or heavy materials. Construction workers often use this area of a truck to haul their supplies to and from jobs, but there are other uses outside of work as well. If a friend or family member is moving from one town to another, a truck with a sizable cargo bed maybe of great service. Beds, furniture and moving boxes will not fit in a car but can easily be transported via a truck's cargo bed. For those who buy covers for the cargo bed, this basically turns it into an extra-large trunk space.

Trucks are heavier than smaller automobiles and allow a higher point of view on the road. The field of vision may help avoid accidents in the first place, but if an accident does occur, the largeness of a truck may deter any major injury. The height of the truck also keeps the vehicle from acquiring too much damage if colliding with another automobile (the smaller the car, the greater the damage). Trucks are not invincible, however. So remember to always drive defensively on the road and always wear a seat belt.

Disadvantages

Trucks contribute to air, noise and water pollution as automobiles. Trucks may emit lower air pollution emissions than cars per pound of vehicle mass, although the absolute level per vehicle mile travelled is higher and diesel particulate matter is especially problematic for health. With respect to noise pollution, trucks emit considerably higher sound levels at all speeds compared to typical car. This contrast is particularly strong with heavy-duty trucks. There are several aspects of truck operations that contribute to the overall sound that is emitted. Continuous sounds come from tyres rolling on the roadway, and the constant hum of their diesel engines at highway speeds. Less frequent noises, but perhaps more noticeable, are things like the repeated sharp-pitched whistle of a turbocharger on acceleration or the abrupt blare of an exhaust brake retarder when traversing a downgrade. There has been noise regulation put in place to help control where and when the use of engine braking retarders are allowed.

Concerns have been raised about the effect of trucking on the environment, particularly as part of the debate on global warming. In the period from 1990 to 2003, carbon dioxide emissions from transportation sources increased by 20 per cent, despite improvements in vehicle fuel efficiency.

TRUCKS

Trucking industry

Trucking firms are the link between the consumer and manufacturers. These trucking companies are contracted by businesses to pick up goods, transport them and deliver a wide variety of products that we as consumers rely on all the time. Each of these steps is carefully orchestrated so that the trucks arrive just in time to ship the goods off to their designated destinations.

The trucking industry began at the turn of the 20th century with the invention of the motorized truck. Motorized vehicles were competition for the railroad industry and became a major factor in the increase of land transportation of goods throughout the United States. The development of fuel also contributed to the increased use of trucks. As motor technology advanced and improved, there was a natural progression for the construction of paved roads. As a result, there were regulations set by the state and federal government that were to be adhered to when moving freight.

Prior to the use of trucks, trains were the most efficient mode of transporting goods because it had the capacity to accommodate bulk. Trucks were initially used to deliver items to remote locations that were inaccessible for the train. The first boom in the usage of trucks occurred during the 1920s. At this time, roads were improving which made delivery locations more accessible. Eventually more durable tyres replaced the rubber tyres and trucks were made larger in order to carry more goods while providing comfort to the driver.

Trucking industry

The first trucks were extremely heavy and had crude mechanisms. Initially, they only provided delivery and hauling to the city. This restriction was due in large part because the trucks could not handle the pothole and unpaved roads. The Automobile Club of America put on the very first United States contest for commercial vehicles; the goal of the test was to examine the reliability, speed and capacity of the truck. Excited by the results of the contest, manufacturers were to meet the demand for trucks and the use of trucks for freight transportation flourished.

The trucking industry as we know it was still in its infancy when the Great Depression hit and a number of trucking companies were forced to close their operations. The companies who survived were able to benefit from the repeal of Prohibition, which also occurred during a time of economic recovery. In 1935, Congress passed the Motor Carrier Act; this act provided structure for the industry.

The Motor Carrier Act set regulations for freight-hauling. The act limited the hours that could be driven. It also mandated the classification of freight that could be carried. The owners of the trucking companies became concerned that the new regulations would compromise their competitive advantage over established rail companies. As infrastructures were improved, driver demand increased and opened up opportunity for new businesses to enter the market.

TRUCKS

The trucking industry is a key player in an economy through the transportation of raw materials, produces and finished goods. Trucks are also vital to the construction industry when large amounts of materials are needed for a project.

Under the regulation of ICC, companies who have for-hire trucks were required to apply for a license if they wanted to enter the interstate markets. The guidelines were strict and licenses were granted only if it could be proven that there was a need for additional capacity. The rates, which used to be an agreement between the trucker and the customer, were put in the hands of bureaus. The rate bureaus are owned and administered by participating carriers. The bureaus job is to analyze costs and initiate pricing standards and competitive rates within the industry. In 1980, Congress put through a trucking deregulation bill. The goal of the bill was to increase competition and this competition resulted in reduced shipping costs for customers.

Prior to 1983, truck size and weight limitations were set by individual states. The federal government pushed for legislation that set limitations on the interstate highway system. In addition to increasing the size and weight limitations on truck, the law also resulted in an increase of the national gas tax and increased fees on the industry. Currently, the trucking industry is responsible for paying roughly half of all state and federal road user taxes.

Famous truck manufacturers

Isuzu

Isuzu Motors Ltd. is a Japanese car, commercial vehicle and heavy truck manufacturing company, headquartered in Tokyo. In 2005, Isuzu became the world's largest manufacturer of medium to heavy duty trucks. It has assembly and manufacturing plants in the Japanese city of Fujisawa, as well as in the prefectures Tochigi and Hokkaidō. Isuzu is famous for producing commercial vehicles and diesel engines. By 2009, Isuzu had produced over 21 million diesel engines, which can be found in vehicles all over the world. Isuzu diesel engines are used by Renault, Opel and General Motors.

Volvo Trucks

Volvo is the second largest producer of heavy duty trucks in the world. There are few countries you can visit where there isn't a Volvo truck on the road.

Based in Sweden, Volvo trucks is a truck manufacturer owned by the Volvo Group. The company currently employs over 22,000 people around the world and has its global headquarters in Gothenburg.

Volvo trucks produce and sell over 100,000 trucks each year. Approximately 95 per cent of the trucks they produce are in the heavy weight class above 16 tonnes. A large proportion of Volvo trucks are manufactured in the USA along with Sweden, Brazil and Belgium.

Both Volvo Trucks and the automobiles produced by the Volvo Group are renowned for their safety record and are considered to be some of the safest vehicles in the world. They are also incredibly reliable and durable.

TRUCKS

Daimler AG

Daimler AG is a German car corporation. It is the thirteenth largest car manufacturer and second largest truck manufacturer in the world. In addition to automobiles, Daimler manufactures buses and provides financial services through its Daimler Financial Services arm. The company also owns major stakes in aerospace group EADS, high-technology and parent company of the Vodafone McLaren Mercedes racing team McLaren Group (which currently is in the process of becoming a fully independent stand-alone corporate entity), and Japanese truck maker Mitsubishi Fuso Truck and Bus Corporation.

Daimler produces cars and trucks under the brands of Mercedes-Benz, Maybach, Smart, Freightliner and many others.

Tata Motors

Tata Trucks are amongst the most sought-after heavy commercial vehicles (HCV) in India. Products of Tata Motors Limited – the largest automobile company in India with a consolidated revenues of Rs. 70,938,85 crores (in 2008-09), Tata Trucks not only outplayed its competitors by its qualities, but also by its services.

Tata Motors is the fourth largest truck manufacturer in the world. Established in 1945, it first rolled out its vehicle in 1954. Since then, more than 4 million Tata vehicles run on the Indian roads. It has its manufacturing units located in various locations across the country including Jamshedpur, Pantnagar, Pune, Dharwad and Lucknow.

Tata Trucks have created a niche in the truck industry worldwide. Tata Trucks also lead in the key medium and heavy truck category with an index of 90 in the segment of Tractor-Trailer.

Famous truck manufacturers

PACCAR Inc

PACCAR Inc is the third largest manufacturer of heavy-duty trucks in the world and has substantial manufacture in light and medium vehicles through its various subsidiaries.

Based in Bellevue, Washington, it was founded in 1905 by William Pigott, Sr., as the Seattle Car Manufacturing Company. Its original business was the production of railway and logging equipment. Upon a subsequent merger with a Portland, Oregon firm, Twohy Brothers, Seattle Car Manufacturing Company became the Pacific Car and Foundry Company.

Pacific Car and Foundry purchased Seattle's Kenworth Motor Truck Company in 1945 and both Peterbilt Motors Company and Dart Truck Company 13 years later. In 1972 the corporate name was officially changed to PACCAR Inc, with the Pacific Car and Foundry Company name being assigned to a division thereof.

MAN SE

MAN SE is one of Europe's leading manufacturers of commercial vehicles, engines and mechanical engineering equipment. The group supplies trucks, buses, diesel engines as well as turbo machinery. MAN SE primarily operates in Europe. It is headquartered in Munich, Germany and employs more than 47,740 people.

The MAN SE Group is one of Europe's leading industrial players in transport-related engineering, with revenue of approximately €14.7 billion in 2010. As a supplier of trucks, buses, diesel engines, turbo machinery and special gear units, MAN SE employs approximately 47,700 people worldwide. Its divisions hold leading positions in their respective markets.

TRUCKS

Some famous trucks

The Terex Titan

The Terex Titan was manufactured by General Motors of Canada. It is the world's largest tandem axle truck ever built to this date. It measures a whopping 20 m long and 6.8m tall. When its dump box is extended, it is capable of standing at 17 m tall, the equivalent of five stories!

The Terex Titan is powered by a 16 cylinder locomotive engine and delivers 3300 horsepower. The cylinder was combined with a huge generator to deliver power to 4 traction engines located on the real wheels. The generator alone has enough power to supply 250 homes with electricity.

Back in 1978, one Titan was brought to Sparwood, B.C. from California, for use in a mine. The truck was too large to be moved by road, so it arrived by train on 8 flatbed cars. It was re-assembled and driven to the mine.

The tyres are 3.5 m in diameter, and weigh 4 tons each. Two Greyhound buses and two pick-up trucks would fit inside its dumper.

The Titan is no longer used because of the huge expenditure needed to keep it running. This truck is a tourist attraction in Sparwood, British Columbia, Canada.

The Terex Titan was first shown to the public in Las Vegas at the American Mining Congress.

Some famous trucks

The Caterpillar 797

The Caterpillar 797 mining truck was the largest of its kind in the world until 2001. Brought into operation in 2000, it has a payload capacity of 360 tons. It is powered by a 24 cylinder V24 quad-turbo diesel engine that produces an amazing 3,400 horsepower. The truck is 7 m from the road to the top of truck bed, and almost 15 m tall when the bed is raised for dumping. The total length of the truck is 14.4 m.

Eight onboard computers monitor oil pressure, transmission torque, engine performance and tyre temperature. The Caterpillar 797 sells for $3.4 million; the 3.9 m tall Michelin tyres were especially designed for the 797, and cost about $30,000 each.

With a full load, the 797 can move as fast as 64 km/h on level ground.

The truck uses fuel in huge amounts, an average of 65 gallons/hr with a fuel economy rating of 0.3 mpg. With such huge costs involved, the vehicle is usually run 24 hours per day, 365 days per year, stopping only for regularly scheduled maintenance.

The DT60 became the most popular engine in heavy duty trucks in the 1990s. This was due to its reliability and fuel economy.

TRUCKS

Liebherr T 282B

The Liebherr T 282B is a large earth-hauling dump truck designed by Liebherr, a German manufacturer of heavy equipment, household appliances, microelectronics, car parts, tool machines and aerospace components.

Launched in 2004, it became the largest earth-hauling truck in the world. The T 282B is an updated version of the T 282 truck. The trucks are assembled in a 10 acre (4 hectare) factory in Newport News, Virginia, USA, that can handle four 282s at a time.

The T 282B has an empty weight of 203 tonnes and a maximum capacity of 365 tonnes. The maximum operating weight is 592 tonnes. It is 14.5 m long and 7.4 m tall over the canopy, with a wheelbase of 6.6 m. The top speed of the truck is 65 km/h.

The truck costs about US$ 3.5 million. A CD-player and air conditioning systems are listed on the optional equipment spec, unusual in the world of professional hauling. Liebherr sells up to a few dozen of them every year, primarily to coal, copper, iron and gold mines in USA, Chile, Indonesia, South Africa and Australia.

> **A salt shaker is a snow plow.** Truckers call the snow plow a salt shaker because of its ability to spread salt on the highways during icy conditions on the highway.

Some famous trucks

Dekotora

Dekotora or Decotora is the local abbreviation for 'Decoration Truck'. They are sometimes known as the Art Trucks too. The truckers of Japan love to decorate their trucks with shiny stainless or golden exterior parts, beautifully painted landscapes, kabuki or manga characters or pictures of celebrities. At night, their fluorescent handiwork comes to life with colourful and bold neon and ultraviolet light displays. These decorations usually adorn the cab as well as the trailer, on the exterior as well as in the interior.

Decotora truck owners are very passionate about the looks of their decorated trucks. They have an emotional attachment with their trucks and do not care about the money they spend in decorating these trucks. What gives them the satisfaction and pride is the personalization and symbolic meaning of these art designs on their trucks. The trucks look like artsy monsters after decoration. Seeing this large scale decoration, anybody could easily confuse these Dekotora trucks to be something art related but automotive. Despite of so much decoration Dekotora trucks still retain their performance ability and are used as reliable workhorses.

Owners of these decorated Japanese trucks often form groups or Dekotora communities. They organize shows to showcase Dekotora trucks and arrange competitions for best decorated trucks.

TRUCKS

Monster Trucks

Known for its extraordinarily big wheels, the monster truck is part of a very popular sports entertainment that is closely associated with other events such as car-eating robots, tractor pulls and mud bogging. Due to the ordinarily massive design of this vehicle, many people are easily attracted to it.

Upon seeing a monster truck, it is very hard to notice its massive tyres, which go very well with its equally large body frame. This type of vehicle uses Terra tyres, each of which measures 1.7 by 1.1 by 0.6 m or 66 by 43 by 25 inches. Its engines have displacement of more or less 575 cubic inches. Aside from these things, it is also important to look at its custom-designed or modified automatic transmission, which makes use of versions like the Ford C6 transmission, the Power glide as well as the Turbo 400.

In terms of design, this kind of truck features a tubular chassis that is custom-built, supercharged engines and modified axles. Likewise, it also has four-wheel steering for better driving control. Trucks with automatic transmissions usually come with heavy-duty gear sets, manual valve bodies and transbrakes.

Although monster trucks run only in small arenas, the safety and well-being of drivers and spectators are highly important. Before drivers can participate, they need to wear head and neck restraints, helmets and safety harnesses. To prevent them from burning in case accidents arise, they are also required to use fire suits.

> **The world's largest monster truck is Bigfoot 5. It weighs 17236 kg and stands a giant 15 ft 6 inches tall, sporting 10 ft tall Firestone Tundra tyres.**

Test Your MEMORY

1. What are trucks?

2. Write briefly about the history of trucks.

3. Name the types of trucks.

4. What are the parts of a truck?

5. Write briefly about truck maintenance.

6. What are the advantages of a truck?

7. What are the disadvantages of a truck?

8. Write briefly about the trucking industry.

9. Name two famous truck manufacturers.

10. Write briefly about Isuzu truck manufacturers.

11. What are Dekotora trucks?

12. What are monster trucks?

Index

B

Battery 17
brake fluid 14
brakes 5, 6, 15, 16

C

cab 3, 6, 10, 11, 12, 29
Cab 10
cargo space 11
Caterpillar 797 27
CB 6
chassis 3, 6, 9, 10, 12, 30
Chassis 10
cockpit 4, 11
coolant 14, 15
crane 13

D

Daimler AG 24
Daimler-Motoren-Gesellschaft 4
Dekotora 29, 31
disc brakes 6
drive gear 11, 12

E

Engine 10

G

Garbage Trucks 8
gearbox 12

H

horsepower 4, 6, 26, 27
hydraulic system 15

I

Isuzu Motors Ltd 23

L

Liebherr T 282B 28

M

MAN SE 25
mirrors 17

O

oil 14, 15, 27

P

PACCAR Inc 25
Pickup Trucks 8
pollution 19
power steering fluid 14

R

Rigid Trucks 7

S

Signals 17
switch 13

T

Tata Motors Limited 24
Terex Titan 26
Tippers 7
Tyres 15, 16
Truck 3, 11, 24, 25, 29
trucking industry 3, 18, 20, 21, 22, 31
turbocharger 6, 19

V

vehicle 3, 4, 5, 8, 9, 11, 12, 13, 14, 15, 16, 18, 19, 23, 24, 27, 30
Volvo Trucks 23